T0070990

NOTE

THIS work was originally designed for broadcasting. For concert and church use, certain modifications are necessary.

This is especially the case in the accompaniment to the Speaker's voice. For broadcasting, this should be performed *poco forte*, but ' faded down' so as to form a background to the voice. In the concert room this must be represented by the softest *pianissimo* so that the Speaker's voice may absolutely dominate.

The soprano part should be sung by a powerful dramatic voice, but there must be no *vibrato.* On no account should the part be sung by a single boy's voice, though in the case of necessity it may be sung by several boys' voices in unison.

The children's part must be sung by real children's voices, not sophisticated choir boys.

The work was originally scored for large orchestra including six trumpets and six clarinets. If necessary, trumpets 4, 5, and 6 and clarinets 4, 5, and 6 may be omitted and, to meet the needs of even smaller resources, the score has been extensively 'cued in.'

Owing to the chronic scarcity of tenors, the tenor line should be strengthened by a few high baritones. Where the tenor line divides, the higher notes should be taken by the real tenors and the lower by the baritones.

ORCHESTRATION
(Reduced Version)

Flutes 1 & 2
Oboes 1 & 2
Clarinets 1 & 2
Bass Clarinet (ad lib)
Bassoons 1 & 2
Double Bassoon (ad lib)
Horns 1 & 2
Horns 3 & 4 (ad lib)
Trumpets 1 & 2
Trumpet 3 (ad lib)

Trombones 1, 2 & 3
Tuba (ad lib)
Timpani 2 (or 3)
may be doubled if another player is available
Percussion (1 Player)
Side Drum, Triangle, Cymbals, Bass Drum
Harp or Piano (ad lib)
Organ (ad lib)
If no Organ, the orchestra should play all Organ cues.
Strings

(Score and Parts available for Rental)

DURATION 15–16 minutes

A SONG OF THANKSGIVING

SOPRANO SOLO AND CHORUS

Blessed art thou, O Lord God of our fathers; and to be praised and exalted above all for ever.
And blessed is thy glorious and holy Name; and to be praised and glorified above all for ever.
Blessed art thou in the temple of thine holy glory; and to be praised and exalted above all for ever.
Blessed art thou on the glorious throne of thy kingdom, and to be praised and glorified above all for ever.

—Song of the Three Holy Children, vv. 29, 30, 31 & 33

SPEAKER

O God, thy arm was here,
and not to us, but to thy arm alone
ascribe we all. Take it, God, for it is none but thine.

—Henry V, Act IV, Sc. 8.

CHORUS

Thine, O Lord, is the greatness, and the power and the glory.
Thine is the victory, and the majesty; for all that is in the heaven and earth is thine.
Thine is the kingdom, O Lord, and thou art exalted as head above all.

—I Chronicles XXIX, v. 2.

SOPRANO SOLO

O give thanks unto the Lord because he is gracious:
for his mercy endureth for ever.

—Song of the Three Holy Children, v. 67

SPEAKER AND CHORUS

The Spirit of the Lord God is upon me, because the Lord hath anointed me to proclaim liberty to the captives and the opening of the prison to them that are bound, to comfort all that mourn; to give them beauty for ashes, the oil of joy for mourning, the garment of praise for the spirit of heaviness.

—Isaiah, LXI, vv. 1, 2, 3

CHORUS

Go through, go through the gates, prepare ye the way of the people; cast up, cast up the highway; gather out the stones.
Lift up a standard for the people.
Behold, the Lord hath proclaimed unto the ends of the world,—say ye, "Behold thy salvation cometh, Behold, his reward is with him and his work before him."
And they shall call them the holy people, the redeemed of the Lord: and thou shalt be called "Sought Out," a city not forsaken.

—Isaiah, LXII, vv. 10, 11, 12

SPEAKER

And they shall build the old wastes, they shall raise up the former desolations.
And they shall repair the waste cities, the desolations of many generations.

—Isaiah, LXI, v. 4

SPEAKER

Violence shall be no more heard in thy land,
wasting nor destruction within thy borders;
but thou shalt call thy walls Salvation, and thy gates Praise.

CHORUS

But thou shalt call thy walls Salvation, and thy gates Praise.

—Isaiah, LX, v. 18

CHILDREN'S VOICES

Land of our birth, we pledge to thee
Our love and toil in the years to be;
When we are grown and take our place
As men and women with our race.

Father in Heaven who lovest all,
O help thy children when they call.
That they may build from age to age
An undefiled heritage.

CHORUS

Teach us the strength that cannot seek,
by deed, or thought, to hurt the weak;
That, under thee, we may possess
Man's strength to comfort man's distress.

Teach us delight in simple things,
The mirth that has no bitter springs;
Forgiveness free of evil done,
And love to all men 'neath the sun.

ALL VOICES

Land of our birth, our faith, our pride,
For whose dear sake our fathers died;
O Motherland, we pledge to thee,
Head, heart and hand through the years to be.

*—Rudyard Kipling**

SOPRANO SOLO

The Lord shall be thine everlasting light,
and the days of thy mourning shall be ended.

—Isaiah LX. v. 20

---

*Reprinted from "PUCK OF POOK'S HILL" by permission of Mrs. George Bambridge.

A Song of Thanksgiving

R. VAUGHAN WILLIAMS

Copyright, 1945, by the Oxford University Press, London.

Printed in U. S. A.

OXFORD UNIVERSITY PRESS • NEW YORK AND LONDON

* Upper stems, Tenor and high Baritone

Sop. Solo
Bless-ed art thou in the tem-ple of thine ho - ly glo - ry;
S. A.
T. Bar. B.
Trombone
Sop. Solo
and to be praised and ex-alt - ed a - bove all for ev - er.
3
CHORUS
S. A.
Bless - ed art thou on the glo - rious throne of thy king - dom,
T Bar.
Bless - ed art thou on the glo - rious throne of thy king - dom,
B.
Bless - ed art thou on the glo - rious throne of thy king - dom,

S.
— and to be praised — and glo - ri-fied a - bove
A.
T.
— and to be praised — and glo - ri-fied a - bove
Bar.
B.
— and to be praised — and glo - ri - fied for
f
all for ev - er, — for ev - er,
all for ev - er, — for ev - er,
ev - er, for — ev — for ev - er,
Ped.

To be spoken– the notaion is purely conventional and does not imply any particular pitch, and need not be in absolute strict time, but must finish at the places where the Orchestra and Chorus swell up.

4

SPEAKER

O God thy arm was here,

S. for ev - - - er, for ev - -

A. for ev - - - er, for ev - er, for ev - -

T. Bar. for ev - - - er, for ev - er, for ev - -

B. for ev - - - er, for ev - er, for ev - -

Spk. and not to us, but to thy arm a - lone as-cribe we

S. - er, for ev - er, for ev -

A. - er, for ev - er, for ev - er for

T. Bar. - er, for ev - - er.

B. - er, for ev - er.

*This is only a 'safety' pause. If the speaker has already reached the last word then go on at once to the next bar.

5
S.
A.
glo - ry. Thine is the vic - to - ry, and the ma - jes - ty; for
T.
Bar.
glo - ry. Thine is the vic - to - ry, and the ma - jes - ty; for
B.
glo - ry. Thine is the vic - to - ry, and the ma - jes - ty; for
cresc.
all that is in the heav'n and earth is thine. Thine is th
all that is in the heav'n and earth is thine. Thine is the
Ped.
king - dom, O Lord, and thou art ex - alt - ed,
king - dom, O Lord, and thou art ex - alt - ed,

6
S.
Thou art ex - alt - ed,
A.
Thou art ex - alt - ed,
T. Bar.
Thou art ex - alt - ed,
B.
Thou art ex - alt - ed,
S.
thou art ex - alt - ed as head a - bove all.
A.
thou art ex - alt - ed as head a bove all.
T. Bar.
thou art ex - alt - ed as head a - bove all.
B.
thou art ex - alt - ed as head a - bove all.
Trumpets
Timpani
Sop. Solo
ff
O give thanks un - to the Lord be - cause he is
fpp

Sop. Solo
gra - cious: for his mer - cy en - dur - eth for ev - er.
Andante sostenuto ♩ = 64
SPEAKER
The Spi-rit of the Lord God is up - on me,
(Organ) p
Piano
Andante sostenuto ♩ = 64
(Strings)
pp
Spk.
be-cause the Lord hath an - oint - ed me to pro - claim li-ber-ty to the captives

Spk.
and the op-en-ing of the pri-son to them that are bound, to
7
Spk.
com-fort all that mourn; to give them
Sop. Semi Chos.
p
pp
to com - fort all that mourn;
3
repeat chord when necessary
Spk.
beau - ty for ash-es, the oil of joy
Sop. Semi Chos.
pp
beau - ty for ash - es,
3
pp

Spk.

for mourn - ing, the gar - ment of praise for the spi - rit of

Semi Chos.

pp

the oil of joy for mourn - ing, the gar-ment of

pp pp

Spk.

hea - vi - ness.

Semi Chos.

praise for the spi - rit of hea - - - vi - ness.

Alla marcia ♩ = 112

f Brass & Harp

3 3

8

T. Bar.

f

Go through, go through the gates,

B.

f

Go through, go through the gates,

SOPRANO & ALTO
T.
Bar.
pre- pare ye the way of the peo-ple; cast up, cast up the
B.
pre- pare ye the way of the peo-ple;
S.
A.
high- way; ga - ther out the stones.
S.
A.
Lift up a stan- dard for the peo-ple.
T.
Bar.
Lift up a stan- dard for the peo-ple.
B.
Lift up a stan- dard for the peo-ple.

9
S. A.
T. Bar.
B.
Lift up a stan - dard for the peo - ple. Be -
Lift up a stan - dard for the peo - ple. Be -
Lift up a stan - dard for the peo - ple. Be -
-hold, the Lord hath pro - claimed un - to the ends of the world,—
-hold, the Lord hath pro - claimed un - to the ends of the world,—
-hold, the Lord hath pro - claimed un - to the ends of the world,—
unis.
Say ye, 'Be -
Say ye, 'Be - hold thy sal - va - tion com - eth,
Say ye. 'Be - hold thy sal - va - tion com - eth,

10
S. A.
-hold, his re-ward is with him and his work be-fore him. And they shall
T. Bar.
And they shall
B
And they shall
S. A.
call them the ho - ly peo - ple, the ho -
T. Bar.
call them the ho - ly peo - ple, the ho -
B.
call them the ho - ly peo - ple, the ho -
8va Bass ad lib.
unis.
S. A.
- ly peo-ple, the redeemed of the Lord:
T. Bar.
- ly peo-ple, the redeemed of the Lord:
B.
- ly peo-ple, the redeemed of the Lord:
con 8va

repeat when necessary)

SPEAKER
And they shall build the old wastes, they shall raise up the former des-o-la-tions. And
S.
pp
thou shalt be called a ci-ty not for-
A.
pp
T. Bar.
pp
thou shalt be called a ci-ty
B.
pp
thou shalt be called
pp
Ped.
Spk.
they shall repair the waste ci-ties, the des-o-la-tions of ma-ny gen-er-a-tions.
S.
-sa-ken, not for-sa-ken
A.
T. Bar.
not for-sa-ken
B.
not for-sa-ken, not for-sa-ken
Ped.

12
Largamente
poco f dolce.
p
S.
Thou shalt be called 'Sought Out' a ci - ty not for - sak - en.
A.
Thou shalt be called 'Sought Out' a ci - ty not for - sak - en.
T. Bar.
Thou shalt be called 'Sought Out' a ci - ty not for - sak - en.
B.
Thou shalt be not for - sak - en.
Largamente
f
SPEAKER
Vi - o-lence shall be no more heard in thy land, wasting nor des - truction within thy
pp
Spk.
borders; but thou shalt call thy walls Sal - va-tion, and thy gates Praise.
Ped.

13
S.
A.
T. Bar.
B.
p
But thou shalt call thy walls Sal-va - tion, and thy gates
But thou shalt call thy walls Sal-va - tion, and thy gates
fp
f
Moderato ♩=80
ff
Praise, Praise, Praise.
Praise, Praise, Praise.
Moderato ♩=80
Strgs. & Org.
fp

CHILDREN'S VOICES
Ch.
p
Land of our birth, we pledge to thee Our love and
toil in the years to be; When we are grown and take our
14
place As men and wo - men with our race.
p
Ped.
Fa - ther in Heav'n who lov - est

Chn
all, O help thy chil - dren when they call. That they may
Chn
build from age to age An un - de - filed he - ri - tage.
15
SEMI CHORUS
p
S.
Teach us the
FULL CHORUS p
T. Bar.
Teach us the strength that can-not
FULL CHORUS p
B.

S.
strength that can- not seek to hurt the weak, That, un - der thee,
FULL CHORUS
A.
That, un - der
T. Bar.
seek, by deed, or thought, to hurt the weak; That, un - der
B.
FULL CHORUS
S.
we may pos - sess Man's strength, man's
A.
thee, we may pos - sess Man's strength to com - fort man's dis -
T. Bar.
thee, we may pos - sess Man's strength to com - fort man's dis -
B.

16
S.
strength to com - fort man's dis - tress. Teach us de -
A.
- tress. Teach us de -
T. Bar.
- tress. Teach us de -
B.
Teach
S.
- light in sim - ple things, The mirth that has no bit - ter
A.
T. Bar.
- light in sim - ple things, The mirth that has no bit - ter
B.
us sim - ple things, no bit - - - - - ter

S.
springs; For-give-ness free of ev - il done, And love to all men'neath the sun.
A.
T.
Bar.
springs; For-give-ness free of ev - il done, And love to all men'neath the sun.
B.
f
CHILDREN (and all other available voices)
17
ff
Land of our birth, our faith, our
S.
A.
ff
T.
Bar.
ff
Land of our birth, our faith, our
B.
ff
ff

Chn etc.
pride, For whose dear sake our fa-thers died; O Mo-ther-
O Mo-
S. A.
pride, For whose dear sake our fa-thers died; O Mo-ther-
T.
Bar.
pride, For whose dear sake our fa-thers died; O Mo-ther-
B.
Chn etc.
-land, we pledge to thee, Head, heart and hand through the years
S.
-ther-land, we pledge to thee, Head, heart and hand through the years
A.
-land, we pledge to thee, Head, heart and hand through the years
T. Bar.
-land, we pledge to thee, Head, heart and hand through the years
B.

Maestoso
Ch^n etc.
to be.
S.
to be.
A.
T. Bar.
to be.
B.
Maestoso
ff
18
p
Sop. Solo
The Lord shall be thine ev-er-last-ing light,
pp
Ped.
Sop. Solo
and the days of thy mourning shall be end - ed.
pp (Trumpet)